Advance Praise

"The horses in Lisa Graley's poems could be horses on walls in caves in France. Or Joy Harjo's horses. The steeds of Marcus Aurelius, Peter the Great, or Joan of Arc. Or of the herds of the wild horses of Sable Island. They could descend from Xena's horses, or Demeter's, or Laura Wingfield's precious and breakable treasures. Or come to us from Bucephalus or some blue roan of Arabia, or even the winged Pegasus. But they are none of these. The horses in Graley's *Box of Blue Horses* are all creations of a formidable, brilliant poet who knows expressionistic impulse and its modalities lie at the heart of all art. She knows every story, poem, symphony, painting, or song resides first inside the recesses of thought or soul or psyche and then its job is to express thought or soul or psyche. With this book she will take her place among whatever we come to call artists who follow the likes of Kandinsky and Marc, the de Koonings, Alice Neel and Michael Hafftka, Pina Bausch and Rilke, Tennessee Williams and Djuna Barnes."

 —Darrell Bourque, Louisiana Poet Laureate, 2007-08, 2009-11, and author of *Megan's Guitar and Other Poems from Acadie*

"The poems in Lisa Graley's *Box of Blue Horses* chart the course of lovers. Graley's glass steeds, like those painted by Franz Marc, to whom she pays tribute, nevertheless walk, canter, gallop and resist, as she explores every angle of desire and the courage required to live by it. 'We hold on,' cautions the speaker, 'to the fire channeled through us/ with that blessed dab of grace.' Graley's varied use of syntax, diction and tone creates the electric arc spanning the speaker and her 'burning one,' who's risked releasing the horses from their box. The speaker hangs back, jockeying between watcher/advice giver, and the one who still wishes to 'touch,' 'to be touched.' 'For who,' the speaker challenges her beloved, 'can hold/ a blue herd of horses/unless she box/the shadow of the universe?'"

—Alice Derry, author of *Tremolo* and *Strangers to Their Courage*

"Lisa Graley's strange and beautiful book-length poem, *Box of Blue Horses*, is unlike any other poem I have read and unlike the work of any other poet I know. The richness of her language somewhat suggests Hart Crane's voyages among the adagios of his islands. But her words are more than merely beautiful. They, to use a passage from her poem, 'pummel / the kicking boards of our hearts,' and they do that because they so often can be read in more than one way. She asks 'who can

hold / a blue herd of horses /unless she box / the shadow of the universe?' Does Graley mean *fight* or *enclose*—or both? With each of my readings of this book, Lisa Graley's *Blue Horses* grew richer and more powerful, which is exactly what we demand and expect of the finest poetry."
    —John Wood, author of *The Gates of the Elect Kingdom* and *Endurance and Suffering*

"The uncontrollable Blue Horses, the chase and fever of the ride, their blue longing, 'moon chorus behind' and all that's trodden under, can't be interpreted. Their force sweeps through the poems, rides over us. Visually rich, ekphrastic, Graley's work syncs art and need, passion and confusion. It's a 'perilous trek,' following the maze of the untamable. If 'courage runs high, good sense low,' the crashing and deepening force will unsettle and excite you."
    —Beverly Burch, judge and author of *Sweet to Burn*

Box of Blue Horses

by Lisa Graley

Winner of the Gival Press Poetry Award

Arlington, Virginia

Copyright © 2013 by Lisa Graley.
All rights reserved under International and Pan-American Copyright Conventions. Printed in the United States of America.
With the exception of brief quotations in the body of critical articles or reviews, no part of this book may be reproduced or transmitted in any form or by any means, graphic, electronic, or mechanical, including photocopying, recording, taping, or by any information storage or retrieval system, without the permission in writing from the publisher.

Published by Gival Press, an imprint of Gival Press, LLC.
For information please write:
Gival Press, LLC
P. O. Box 3812
Arlington, VA 22203
www.givalpress.com

First edition
ISBN: 978-1-92-8589-86-0
eISBN: 978-1-928589-89-1
Library of Congress Control Number: 2013948200

Artwork:
1942.1
Franz Marc
The Large Blue Horses
1911
Oil on Canvas
41-5/8 x 71-5/16 inches unframed
Collection Walker Art Center, Minneapolis
Gift of the T. B. Walker Foundation, Gilbert M. Walker Fund, 1942

Author photo by Chelsea Ellison
Design by Ken Schellenberg

Index of First Lines

Lift the lid slowly 1
Who has not loved them 3
Their blue is not cool, ...5
Lovely are the mares 6
The tourists are coming 7
What we can say of them 10
Come this way, I'll show you 13
Where have they gone, the horses. 16
Everywhere the spoor grows weak, ...22
They go in search 23
They return to the caves. 25
They have pulled through, ... 28
There is time left for you 31
And would you still have your ride. 33
This long night I have heard you breathe. 35
Listen, it was I who boxed them, ...37
Headstrong and frenzied, ...41
Smaller and smaller grows 44
What I'm saying, ... 45
Go, now, I have said it, ...47
Why lead us here, this brackish shore, ... 48
What figures are these 50
Down that road I hear them coming 51
To touch or not, ...52
We need no second glance 53
A foal has come 54

Come the days 55
They are, of all things, here 56
These are they once stoked the oven 59
A herd of blue horses 62
If it's box you're weighing. 65
For who can afford in body and soul 67
Coming round to oneself 68
Yet comes in your invariable stall 69
Round us they ring 70
It is just this, that you 71
You have set alight that of your choice. 73
Once upon the back of a blue horse 74
Times there is a getting on, ...76
There are still points off radar. .78
Some days tend toward pilgrimage. 80
Nights I know I've heard the horses 83
Comes comfort in the liniment. 84
Tonight, I sing of blue horses. 86

Acknowledgment

Poem 15 and a portion of poem 16 were published under the title "In Which the Persona Confesses to Boxing the Blue Horses" by *Water~Stone Review* (Volume 14, Fall 2011): 232-233.

1

Lift the lid slowly
—for they are at the gate
throttle down
or up
the direction of increase,
waxing.
You can smell the hay,
manure, piss,
but this scent, too:
bestial.

Inside, they are cornered
four ways
frothing
jostling
eight of them
blue as woe
shiny as glass

their ears bent back
by wind,
inquisitiveness,
arousal.
They are fierce.
It is ache,
ignition.

Lift the lid higher
—just barely so—
tilt the box
slightly—for better light—
see them straining
hear them panting
feel the steam of their lathered heat

—but wait, you have gone too far—
eight come tumbling out
sturdy on glass legs
rushing bucking
they splinter the cedar box,
snap what nets you've spun.
Neck and necking
they gnash their bits in half.
Their faces blaze.
They are thirsty and drinking,
they are hungry and eating,
they are racing and bleeding,
sowing oats
kicking up
dust you are and dust
they will run you over
press you flat
level in their field.
They will crush you.
Come, my burning one,
no way to herd them.
They will not go back.

2

Who has not loved them
blue in their pasture
more grosbeak than bunting
—and so, greater the rub?

Who has not loved
their gentleness in pasture
drowsy and grazing
their tongues sweet with clover
and the slow, munching chomp
nudges them towards
and away from
one another?

Who has not reached in sleep
for the tangled neck of one,
the mane to come comb-handed,
pulse and breath to flare
the pressure of a finger?

Who has not dreamed the ghost ship
—bluest white you can picture—
trawling the salt-peppered shark loop
completes its circuit there?
Dreamed the horizon from the bow
—Ithaca, my friends, Indies,
Canaan-whet,

terra cognita,
terra desiderabile?

And who has not loved them
astonishing on the beach
their hooves sunk wet in sand
when first you steady them
in scope and imagination?

I have loved them, too, my friend,
and dreamed of setting sail,
orange or carrot in hand,
complimentary offering,
but what tales I've heard
drive me back
to where I'm standing.

3

Their blue is not cool,
not the blue of slate nor sea swell
but hot entirely.
It is fire
beguiling goblin
you've read about
seizes the ocular circuitry
salts the molten ores,
heats the copper seam running
sternum to pudendum.

It is better the blue of ink perhaps
in old ballpoints and squid
(more this than ocean)
spilled and unscripted
siphoned from that tight straw
draws us
to bursting
then stains
the pocket
pants or shirt
wherever we happened to stash it.
There's too much pressure in the cabin, sir,
who is it can contain it?

4

Lovely are the mares
and their shudders
lovely the blue mares.

5

The tourists are coming
in threes and fours—
somebody's selling tickets
nonrefundable bargains
half-offered, zero interest.

If you must look—
look from a respectable distance
—reason for the zoom—
what more is granted anyhow
than sight of breast, shoulder, croup,
withers, flank, and stifle—
all identified this far back
—though famously untouchable?

Pan your camera
one end to the other
find this one swatting her tail
swinging her head to clip the fly
that's pinched her rounded rump.
And three nearby are cropping grass
their backs thrown to the buzz
and chatter, shutters snapping, usual banter
that follows horses torn from boxes.
Another lies, her legs enfolded,
pallet indulged by midday sun.
And over here—two are merging

forehead to forehead
in slack-lipped nip and nuzzle
velvet to velvet
wet knead.

Had you patience
(and a head for reckoning)
you could have
slipped down the ladder
slid onto the back of one
—not that one—she is foaling—
gone for a private ride
inside the box,
got off where you got on
instead of loosing the whole lot.

But that is over now
—nothing gained in blaming—

They are bundled
and will not separate.
And you—you will fall
short of naming them.
You will not distinguish among them.
It is need for all, not part,
what will drive you from now on.

Inch closer you like,
but keep back of the rocks

—your fear they sense
in sleight of nostril
tuned and tuning to the wind.
Their stiff ears cup your slow crawl
—till there is sudden quake
the earth jarred under palms and knees
rippling upwards, arms and thighs
racking suspension
your back that rickety bridge
coccyx to pith to steering mechanism.
The horses snort and humph,
they rear and stamp and thump
and with the force of their forelegs
chisel half moons in the dirt
as those coming to sudden stops
will telegraph warning:
lands posted,
hands off.

6

What we can say of them
they have been honest from the get-go
and hurled no smokescreen.
How will you then proceed?
What was it you expected?

Their business is bruising,
hoof-beating, bullying,
ancient grind of bone and gristle
split shins and shattered patellae,
you can't hope
to stay unscathed—
better grab your chaps
next time you come
whatever leather you brought
—and cleats—
for some toehold in this world.

What was it, you said, your intention?

I would like to see
your hand there,
cannot hope but wish it
dangerous game
you play
and not the one
most likely for it.

What chance have you in the open field?
None I can see or know of.
What is it gives you boldness then
to climb the awkward stare
and scale the wordless spaces
as one conditioned to height
will go without a net?
You've never been and cannot be
the vaulter of that vision.
What is it gives you boldness then,
where comes the pluck and mettle?
Are you good with rope—that the trick?—
braiding, knotting, throwing?
How are you with rope
(just a question)
roped in and into, over,
and under? On your back,
drums rolling,
boom falling,
train barreling,
bell tolling,
toll exacted
paltry white threads exposed?
How are you with rope,
just a question.

What I mean,
you shouldn't have let them go
in the first place:

there can be no freedom for both
for the one is slave to the other,
this, the nature of being,
adventure of living so near the stables
—and the blue horses, given rein to run,
will outstrip you every time.

7

Come this way, I'll show you
where they broke through,
the box that held them,
now kindling, you may call it,
a few scraps to build a coat rack,
some decorative table,
bookmarks to memory.

Note the fine cabinetry
—traces in the rubble—
dovetailed corners tabbed
as good cigar boxes built-in
hinges that somehow
account for heat and
swelling brass hardware
tarnished sound through
and through tongue
and groove solid from cedar
one of the sturdier—
a full inch thick
not milled to less
but seasoned some years
before boarding.

Point being, this wasn't some craft box
children tote home from school
but real wood, quarter-sawn,

kind you fell wide trees for
went into this thing
to hold them here.

You will want pictures, documentation,
evidence of how things used to be.
Look all you like, not apt to find
structural defect. Wasn't the corners
gave way but wall—wood itself
and what they saw enticing them,
a smidgen of silage
worth risk of life and clan.

Imagine the muscled will
to break from such cribbed bondage,
knotted soreness, head and knee,
cannon and breastbone, what parts
took the brunt of crashing:
inevitable the pain of rupture,
whether sudden or longed for,
splintering of soul
to find light and air and open range
—and then that slow hatch of knowledge
always comes with hazard gambled.

The wood is storied
in every grain, a tale,
(I have been this morning reading)
seasons of rain and no rain,

years of ant and moth habitation.
The gray rust of weather mere skin
to cover what copperleaf interior
we find and writing everywhere:
all things having things
to tell us
and pasts that accumulate meaning
only with sharing:
stunted limbs and knots
and forks, the rub of antlers
and scent of roe.
Listen, it's understandable
if you want to go back,
don't want to take part.
There's not much salvageable
if you thought to start again.

The crew is here to finish the job
—demolition the horses began.
Take a souvenir, you like,
whatever you fancy.
There will be a pyre
and fire set to the wood.
This is the box some Jack built,
these the beans he scattered;
this the stalk he hoped to climb,
this the stalk to suck dry
in old age.

8

Where have they gone, the horses
frocked in their blue longing,
ones we fired in kilns,
began as sparks, grew up to flame?
Burned for years, then went out,
left us in cold shadow. Flown off
while we were occupied,
had little ground for dwelling
where fodder lay trampled
and constant pacing furrowed paths,
left fields once sunned in sunken.

Where have they gone, the horses
used to trot out their toy boxes
their enticements and seductions
sprint that tempted tender hearts
and spurred us to their backs in sport?
Had been one at every bus stop,
one at every crossing,
and hours of fair play in the stalls
whim in every corner
and in every corner
ore long sought—and water.

How they charged outside the windows
full of storm and fever
compelled you rush through meals

and chores, flashing reds and yellows
pressed you come
on board, you timed it right,
room for one, ticket please,
here the itinerary, here your passport,
here the map strewn with landmarks
only you can interpret.

Where have they gone, the swift steeds
used to wing their way with me
foamy in the chase, essence keen
as wild spring onions trodden under hoof
hurdling hedges, hurdling ditches
well-oiled motion in traffic moving
southside bridge lights the city streaming
and river and river and river below
surefooted piano and banjo out back
and fabulous vertiginous ballooning
bulleting galloping the quickening forge
breathless and heady and panting
no leap too long no creek too deep
no heat too fast no mid-lope doubt
no one saying no
and the sun going down, going down.
Splashing of hooves in the muddy puddles
and all that sandy wash back on you:
exuberant outlaw at best transitory
but where are they now, the horses for racing,
blue streaks on the horizon?

And where have they gone, the trail mounts
used to cross the rocks and desert,
them that sported staying power
whose hooves were scuffed getting there.
You rode them hard
shouldering on, shouldering on
leather gripped, ribs clutched tight
miniscule grit in teeth and eyes
the glutes straining.
There were times
you thought they'd drag you
to death, so headlong
the rush and desperate
the drive in the in-country
where the solo rider
ventures alone.

You rode them with hounds howling
a full moon chorus behind
but not just that—
something out there to get to
shimmering in the sand
undulating, shifting focus
—but scented out, the horse you rode
and for days, weeks, the same talk,
same pauses, same unslaked thirst,
same empty plains, sidewinder trails,
obelisks circled, hospitality of the nomads,
chicory and bergamot in your cup.

You cantered and galloped and jumped
rubberbended the zigzag paths,
shucked off your clothes
fording the streams.

Out of necessity, not just desire
(as if desire were not enough)
you rode to get from here to there
—for detour off the map
forbidden range, forbidden bower.
You rode them bare or saddleback
lacking provision, save what tent
or bivouac you conjured on the ride.
You rode to slay the dragon,
that insatiable dragon,
to capture what chimeras you could.
You rode with sinewed longing
muscled hope, for desert bread,
for union.
You rode to see for yourself
and came back with pockets empty
—and memories thick as web.

And where are they, the other ones,
backwards walkers, tricksters,
mystery ladies, crept up
while you weren't looking
checked your pockets
made off with not just huckleberries

but pieces of you, hand and heart?
Ones that reared and danced
and piggybacked, circus stooges?
Or them that bore the load
where load there was to bear?
Where have they gone, the horses,
witnesses to your calling,
blind seers that once led the way?

Where are the stampedes used to rattle the loft?
Now we do well for a bump in the road.

And where have they gone, my sauntering ones,
them that lagged behind
and by their languor and rippling sway
lured us halting
to still water?
Where we drank our fill and lay beside them
paced to slow and slower dreams.
Theirs was pull of a different power
(the clouds caught up and passed us).
Hypnotic lull, unhurried roam,
slackened reins, loosened bridle,
generous carriage, unfolding warmth
and all about, the current meanders
and reverie light as water lilies
drifts and woos, drifts and lingers,
the long straw down, petals yielding.
Where are they of that winding caravan,
them that slowed us down to grazing?

Where are the blue horses
boxed up for a better day?
Love or fear it was compelled us
bury them, our equine store
like *terra cotta* statuary
for encounters down
the long road to eternity.
Are they cold and hard now
hollow in the grave?

Some days I think I glimpse
the charge far off between the mountains
and hear that rumble rock cascading,
but then a silence
great as death
swallows it.

9

Everywhere the spoor grows weak,
sand blown over,
weeds sprung back,
steady petrification of manure.
Was moons ago, maybe years
last they sifted through.

But here, in ancient oxbow lakes
riparian clay bears the blue print
of their indenture, and here,
the rutting of their hooves
once channeled potable water.

The bur-scrag bark of trees
and nests of sleeping birds
confirm an occasional blue tuft
of horsehair, bleached white now
like denim in the sun.

Somewhere sweaty horse scent
rides frayed on the wind.

10

They go in search
of virgin fields where sap
still springs in spears and stalks
of timothy and brome.

Or to the bogs
to eat the grass
near the peat trains
till race day.

Where someone will notice
and ask them to waltz
offering oats from calloused hands.

They go in search of transport.

They go in search of new riders
and copulation

father for their children
but not just that

someone to curry and coax
from them their quivers
and their arrows.

They go in search of farriers,
and fletchers for their wings.

They go where children
straddle mops and skip
through rodeo dreams.

They flee to dark woods
where shards of light penetrate
and paint them piebald.

They go to the wild
and nest among sleeping deer.
They scratch their rumps on low-lying limbs.

They go to tongue the salt bricks.

They go to blue cities.
They go to blue ports.
They go to blue laws
and blue jokes.
This is the truth.

They go as those
having no place to go
step from pictures
into 3-D then back
to flat monotony.

They go as blue vapor.
We may not see them again.

11

They return to the caves
to the beginning
where the mad limner
binds them to stone
blood, spit, urine
strokes them
horsehair and tendon
daubs them
azure-flecked confetti.

The mad limner
traces their comings
and goings, blows
and bellows their agony,
and what is not blown
is chewed and swallowed.
It is grated travail,
copper lamentation.
You shiver the taste
too wonderful to know
and too much to bear.

He draws them back
in states of becoming,
sheathed suspiration
in form and no form.
They emerge and recede
reined in and reigning.

The blue horses are born
to die over and over
in dark, in moist
in cavern's point and pistil
in never-ending rise,
in womb
(in womb itself generous)
in drip drip action
in never-ending nurture
in milk from silken, earthen teats
wholly fortified.

The limner threads
his hand through
stretchingward the cord
to the other side.
What is there,
we cannot know,
what is there,
we cannot see,
what is there
posted under
lost and found
and through the ages
and eventual strata
waiting rightful owners.

The blue horses are old
as our desire for them

and fraught
with near as much burden.

12

> after Franz Marc's *Tower of Blue Horses*

They have pulled through,
pieces of themselves

merged, slivered
as through cracked mirrors

daring with their gaze
the pierce of blue and black

and cadmium red
anyone to follow.

They have mounted
defense, hackles raised,

blue tower of them
interlocked, layered,

riderless horses from
an apocalypse

they had hoped
to avoid.

They have escaped
in piecemeal armor

once thought flameproof
impermeable

a nose singed here,
an eye there

blood flowing
to the knees and hocks.

They are on the march
blue storm of them

shards drawn tight
branded cross and crescent

away from the testing fire
and arrows

shredded
but still walking.

On the move, blue-bladed pack
keen to the swallowed light

glows in their bellies
and foreheads,

they are flaked
with suspicion

under the single blood-strung bow
that promises no more.

13

There is time left for you
not to waste time
tracking them now the knot
has slipped and chance
to corral them cooled
like the hearths we sat at young.
Nothing to do but pack your sparks
and tiny candles diminishing.
You must not see it as end
but beginning,
to boast clean hands
and feet, prospect
to live without the tow
that all your life
kept you the verge of ruin.

It's true I wanted to sit and watch.
It's true I wanted to watch you.

What they say, what I've heard
you've got horse in you,
blood from times before
descended I guess the days of centaur
especial blend of might and ease
refined habit of looking one way,
going another.
That you'll stride into quarry or ring

without whip or saddlery
and by voice and gaze alone
calm the waters
riots in breasts of untamed ones,
melt the hardened glaze that shelters
from too much—too much.

But then set to rush that which you choose
fistfuls of mane, and symphysis blooming
raptured obscenities whispered around
ironing out what stutter and rage
you have to, clutching femora
and medial malleoli.

Would that these would go down so easily
you could swallow them in a gulp
and earn a smalty feather for your cap,
but the blue horses, could you find them,
have grudges, I don't mind saying,
and long scores to thrash about.

I will not send you the road I've been
or used to dream of going
(stasis the path now chosen)
but will direct you the definite route
leads to the sails and mallemuck
return passage to your home.

14

And would you still have your ride
your stunt, your seventh course,
your ways and questions fielded?
Reckless strut matched zest for zest?

Dare to chart a starbound trek,
embark the perilous trail
after I've said you cannot win
not with what you're dealt
and all that insurmountable bluff
between us and them?
Would you dare toast the sky
cup to the rim, sheer cropping,
cross the canyon without pass
or code or means to cross,
without cover of night
or cover of trees
or someone covering?
Dare demand the prize
that brought you here,
trust your compass face of all
impossibles, dog the avenue
that at every corner re-
routes you dead
end wrong
way no left
turn no

turn
around no
entry no
exit.

Courage runs high, good sense low,
sunrise in the young reason enough
to burrow till sapping passes
and estivation makes starving palatable.

How long can you be held
from scorching the plain
thick in the heat of your hunt?
I'm half a mind to keep with you
but half a mind to turn the other way.

15

This long night I have heard you breathe
and felt your breath upon my shoulder,
close as we've come to trading secrets.
This night I have dreamed the horses
in their droop-eyed sleep and long lashes,
standing in the meadow, and looked
for sleep in you of the kind dammed hearts
will fight and finally give in to.
I have dreamed you, pursued and pursuing,
and heard you whisper in an unknown tongue.

What bread I've broken you've tasted
and know without looking the contents
of the burlap sack, nothing noble
or inspiring there. We carry
our wounds and murders with us,
odd bags of bones and maps
where we meant to be this time next year
divining rods and withered seedlings,
lodestone and flint, leftover charcoal,
whatever leather we used to use
petrified now and crumbling.

What I haven't said, you've heard,
what I haven't opened
you've weighed in hand.
The figure not revealed,

the one you've calculated
and chosen. Maybe truth
would wear a different color
did you not press so steady
your lambent gaze.
across the open grate.

16

Listen, it was I who boxed them,
boxed the blue horses,
boxed and shunned them
with the same heat
I once desired and loved them.

For you must know, I did once
desire and love them.

But was tired of their stink
and briggity prance
and everywhere I stepped, a pile.
Consider the burden
on blistered hands, rope burns
from the inevitable tug and warring.
Bruised metatarsi, just another thing.
Plus, the old bin of rusty shoes
wouldn't no one ever throw away.

Then there was the awful fever
what no one could cure
something in the blood
burrowed under the skin
but rooted deeper, too,
took hold and robbed of sleep,
of waking hours, the same.
A spell of sorts, all anyone can claim.

Was always the threat of collapse
I mean, of breaking out,
and venture against the headwind,
one-way passage
without guaranteed return.

Say, you grew up
knowing what it was
the barn next door
staring through cracks
eye meeting eye
shift and coy
always wishing
the caged beasts yours.

Maybe the horses
were hobbled
too often, curbed
with the short ropes
people give
the ones they love.
Locked down,
seized up, kept
from light of day
and circulation,
fatted so they
couldn't run.

Fine the line, it's been said,
between taming and crippling.

Say, you slipped one time,
swung open the door
the way the young will do.
In the blur of midair
you spun a Ferris fortune
took a ride on the carpet,
learned it wasn't the magic
you thought but twisting
torturous, woven from nightmare
anguish-strung.

Every day wearing the demand
for more: feed and field, sure,
but sacrifice and daring, the same.

A while you can keep that up
breathless fantasy you're wedded to,
hoisted state, night or dawn
but gait impossible to sustain.

Say, one day you give it all
—the next you don't
not without loss—great loss
—till the day they feel you
hesitate in the saddle,

lean back and take
the easy route home.

The blue horses,
what can they do
but despise
and mock you
from then on?

17

Headstrong and frenzied,
they pull one way,
you another,
and carry on so
you can do nothing
but beat them,
yet no matter the welts
bitter the business
flies on open wounds
they will not go under
but pretend half a heart
stuck in your path
like mules instead.

And the thing you love
you hate in the day to day of it.
From me you'll get nothing more.
I've forced, and been forced,
and will, no doubt, and be again.
You remember the direction
against the grain best
that which dulls
your saws and sandpaper.

You whip them into service
goad them to plow straight
years of that, and what

lacerations you heap
are heaped back on you
till you would trade
or sell if they weren't tethered
in ancestral dreams,
mosquito-mingled
their blood with yours
impossible to kill
though neglect is, I warrant,
its own murder.

And one day, maybe you will—
whether by purpose or accident,
it little matters now—
be left with only eight
whose eyes you cannot coax
to any peaceful setting,
whose throats betray
no fond nicker for you
and so you build a box
dovetail the corners
polish bolts and brass
drill air holes,
secure all with galvanized screws,
sturdy enough
for permanence,
all twisted tight,
and countersunk,
every nail clenched

the backside.

The horses will not duck down
without bones broken
(yours and theirs together)
to that half-suffocating dark,
unadorned dungeon.

You must shrink them to fit.
You must reduce, and reduce
your idea of them, and simply forget
any of it that ever was.

18

Smaller and smaller grows
the box that hems them
till you can lock them
under the rolled rim of oak
that domes your desk
and from your window
view again unclouded horizon.

Till you can pass the barn
without tripping
the thin shadows
once snared and fettered you.

For years they may lie there
panting in the dark,
their glow, a secret life.

Till someone comes along,
half-hitched dreams
to ride them, finds them
rib-racked and scabbed,
yet just enough coal left
to catch fire and explode.

19

What I'm saying,
I won't take hold,
no longer the drive
to follow and light
the saddleless back,
no longer the grip
to seize the wheel,
what braided feathers
ornament the mane,
nor even heart enough
to see them again.

Not the box of gears
or amps or nerve it takes
to give them lead
without parachute,
life vest, roll bar,
and all the padding
protects the heels
and kidneys.

Nor no skep deep enough
to hold the mounds of dread
have come to corrupt
the proverbial stalls.

Not the rack of trust to sit them
through glade and thicket

across fault lines, slaloming
among the daisy poplars,
or skimming whitecaps
off some distant skerry.
No hand for soothing
when they bristle and rear,
careen the razorcliff, rockstop gaps
their sights on otherworldly damsels
rubescent novices, all that starry lot.

I had days of that, and they are lost
slipped like melon seeds
from a soft and yielding center,
fell to no soil at all but to creek,
and washed to the edge
of a foreign shore.

20

Go, now, I have said it,
take your liberties, or death.

21

Why lead us here, this brackish shore,
white-washed sand with shadows circling,
rock-rimmed but for the brink
where the round of sea lunges in?

Nothing to say, hasn't been said.
Not the way home, nor the way back.
But like nothing, nonetheless, ever was.

No remnant of box nor timber to build
but only the fetching and receding tide,
a few oxidized coppers of the early years,
antiquated graffiti on the rocks.
Plenty on the coast to startle the heart,
but no track of anything I recognize.

Why have you yoked me thus lightly
rocked in the swing of your lariat?
I've seen your work, your tack and sway,
them that come ambling home.
I've seen you dressed, and undressing,
and know with fair certainty
the edge where your boots wear thin.

From you I expected something more.
From you I expected the fine wrangling
that's been boasted,

bends the will of ironclad ones,
leaves them panting in the dust,
firmness blinked by stress and strain.
From you I expected the fierce hold
comes in grappling for the upper hand.

22

What figures are these
filtered through brume,
tempered by sun and saltwater?

The horses are storming,
times we can feel them
though our eyes be blinded
by white sheets changing shape
in the wind and sand.

23

Down that road I hear them coming
faradic drum of their footfall falling,
filling our pockets, their thundering hum.
Throttled beat, their syncopation
fretting arch to span to dorsal root.

Down that road I see them coming
tousled manes, blue-breached horizon,
bunched up like beads can't nobody string,
just broke through that needle of vanishing point
to rip the stalwart seam.

Across the open beach they bear down,
eyes like black marbles, nostrils flaring,
ears pressed flat and glassy backs
glistening in the sun.

They drag their fire behind them,
stirred up in billows, it flames behind them.
You can feel the burn from here.

24

To touch or not,
to be touched or not,
to meet
where makes
that precipitous turn

when they are near
so near we feel their heat

through ribbons of fog
along the seabed's lacy edge.

25

We need no second glance
to see past ticks and rain rot:
not much plainness about them
for in every forelock and wink
some ember glows.

Up close, blue flair runs ragged
down their hide-bound slopes,
pools at their hooves, a former glory.

Legs that once carted and packed
bear the scars and thorns of mayhem.
What once sallied is sullied,
what once was is wrecked.

Yet for all this, their contours
still move me, quarters round
and stout as the orbiting earth
that withstands our wavering
into and out of the seasons.

26

A foal has come
among them now
all leg
and frolic
and blue
like the rest
wide-eyed
quick-skitting
any direction
direct opposite
a threat:
the rolling
tide, of course,
but even
the zipping
dragonflies,
even the wind-
tipped
goldenrod.

Woolly, too,
that foal,
as any fledgling.

27

Come the days
like yellow leaves of poplars
dropping mid-summer
when you want once more.

There's plenty of give when you fold
and pocket them,
or wad them tight in your hand.

28

after Franz Marc's The Large Blue Horses

They are, of all things, here
where last we saw them
huddled in ways we can't enter

their eyes turned inward
to the light
suffusing them.

To be sure, they are blue
but for the red blush of barrel
reflecting the round, alizarine hills
reflecting them.

And *they* are round
but for their angular noses
and pointed ears,

ears pitched back perhaps
for the soul's loving draw
across the cello's strings.

Round, I say, like
buttocks are round
or the top halves of hearts,

echoed in mustachioed frowns
and the bushy brows of tails and manes
enclosing them.

Closed, I say, their eyes to us
while they preen, groom, curry
scratch a chin

their eyes turned inward
to the light within,
huddled in ways we can't enter.

Huddled against hot hills,
lanceolate leaves,
a sliver of near-sympathetic sky,

they are wholly absorbed
in themselves, steadfast
in their blue business,

in blue as luminous
as it is impenetrable.

And yet, they sense our presence,
are not oblivious to our plight
but have chosen neither nod nor nicker

but to go on without us,
their eyes turned inward
to the scrolling hum of horsey stuff.

They command our gaze,
refuse that our eyes stray far.

We see them for what they are,
bare as they were made, heartbeat
away from enough.

29

These are they once stoked the oven
brought up the sun

dragged it across the dome of sky
whose hooves could touch or not

tilled the whim of castle growers
went between this world and that

carried the dead a final stage
milled their whirring secrets

into buggy flour, sacked
and stacked a forgotten corner.

These are they tricked the sons of Troy
toppled his topless towers

delivered the sea god his biscuits
ushered his cart between the isles

dispersed disease and ample doom
from armored grocery bags.

These are they delivered missives
come back to have their say, their *own* say

chewed through strings to get here
(could have gone through padlocks)

pressed their vantage in lateral work
to checkmate from the blind side.

These are they that were backed long ago
backed by all the big names

staked in races, staked in fields,
staked their lives to ours

must have had molasses pre-run
for the fire that stokes their boxes.

These are they of the early years
when quiet assurance

was all was needed
a whinny for your thoughts

to turn the head, to turn the key
to set most any cogwheel turning.

These are the ones once spotted pastures
plodded paths and crops

stripped the bark from birch trees
bowed saplings down for belly-scratching

pawed earth for copper, and pummeled
the kicking boards of our hearts.

30

A herd of blue horses
standing at ocean's fringe,
one leg each cocked in sleep.

***

I know what it is
to cast the net,
come up straining
with nothing save phantoms
shimmering in tidal pools.

***

The blue horses shiver,
salt-spray of wind
akin to erosion.

***

The sun behind them
their own shadows startle,
they stir and spook.

***

A reach like that of tentacles
from glowing cuttlefish,
the blue horses nibble
the worn frame
of my divided mind.

⁂

They shake the foamy grasp
of the tide increasing.

⁂

Your eyes turned only
toward the blue horses,
your fingers make silent work
knotting the hackamore.

⁂

What is it rattles the dishes,
bobbles the teacups
long-stored in the cupboard?
Is it the blue horses again?

⁂

Manes in the wind,
blue slicing fins
sundering the then
from now.

⁂

A herd of blue horses
a bottle of wine,
but nothing more.

⁂

I heard in midrib
what you said

of the blue horses
but cannot comment
so soon. Not now,
before your words
take root and spread
their viney tendrils.

***

The blue horses
have come to perch
in the branches
of the great oak,
quite the bouquet
of capillaries.
I am bowed down
under the weight of them.

***

Please keep your dreams
quiet, murmured
only to the blue horses.

31

If it's box you're weighing
(and box it ought to be)
I've stashed hammers and hatchets,
brown bags of galvanized nails
twelve-penny, fourteen-,
even block and tackle,
and besides have drawn up
blueprints, sample diagrams,
dimensions to scale,
a manual of instructions
—call it recommendations, you will—
all these I've tucked
back of my haversack
in case—just by coincidence—
we catch sight of these
pan-flash luminescents.

And now that we're here,
dizzied precipice of jeopardy,
it's time to trade beach for timber,
and lay off land for building
—stockade or redoubt—
whatever will stand fixed
to keep them at bay.

Otherwise, let us part
and jot this venture down

as exercise solely
scenic jaunt
and way to stretch
the legs and heart,
means by which to measure
the singular heft
between valor and folly.

32

For who can afford in body and soul
the stock and store of their far roaming?
Who from home to go, from kin and crop,
swaps skeleton key, crooked chimney,
the autumn brilliance of marigold
for dry canteens, miscreant tribes,
rattlesnakes gone berserk,
and firkins empty of ale?

Depends, I guess, what worlds
you're in habit of straddling,
keenness, too, of the creep
of slip-knot desperation.

But say we tarry and follow,
win them round at last,
net a scrap of trust from them,
it's only days, weeks at best
no matter the handler you are,
till they turn and throw us
(inevitable that treacherous blow)
and bite and tear and trample,
abuse us with their coffin bones,
in a land remote, uncharted,
and you, my darling, my delightful one,
will get up and go without me,
the way, they say, of protean charmers.

33

Coming round to oneself
refugee in a badland shelter,
overhead circling
the yellow-beaked crows,
falcons, too, after their share
who can curb the bitter flavor,
the tight-reined thought
what for?

Then to that rocky lowland
of the heart's stubborn fold
paddock not for rent or sale
I will return
no herd in tow

for who can hold
a blue herd of horses
unless she box
the shadow of the universe?

34

Yet comes in your invariable stall
nature's own breaking point,
tip whetted too fine to stand
much friction, match point
peak of phosphorescence
ignited by horses
charging the strand.

Brings us to the point of boiling
or melting, what fire they feed
with driftwood and hot blood
and whatever stubble we've let lie.

Would be the point of saturation
if we fell in, got washed in it,
and stained indigo.

35

Round us they ring
a blazing carousel
nine of them
blue as winning
racking, trotting,
loping—an occasional capriole—
effectual gyroscope
of their own devising
too fast spinning
for stable footing
too fast spinning
too long
enduring
the force
of their
pulling
pure
centrifugal.

Negative or positive valence,
it little matters now
under this heat
and pressure
to succumb.

36

It is just this, that you
reach and in that instant's reaching
catch hold of the one
about to blow by you
no second glance,
and mount the winged steed
outward bound you know not where.

You reach and in that instant's reaching
speed me toward the withers,
and one more time I'm left to seize
the fiery mane and clench my legs
snug as any surcingle, recollecting
in every cell and branch
the familiar *cauda equina*.

We give in, the best
we remember, let go
and gain, in full flexion,
what haste and height
believed lost forever

because, listen, maybe second chances
are like turtles, slick-backed
concealed besides
surfacing you can't tell when.

One more time the round earth falls
away, spun from the hooves
shoving off it. We hold on
to the fire channeled through us
with that blessed dab of grace
somehow got snagged
the hem of our shirttails
just as we made our move.

37

You have set alight that of your choice
and tied me the back of the blue horse

before you, lashed in such fashion
I cannot be tossed nor

change direction, nor lessen the pace
you've fervently pressed.

Neither may I dismount nor take lead
locked in the cradle

of your design: for you have surrounded
me yourself and fueled

fire on the back of the blue horse.

38

Once upon the back of a blue horse
a balancing
begins

for she is eager to move
without us,
and we must negotiate

her switchback turns,
brace ourselves
the dive she thinks will throw us.

Once upon the back of a blue horse
full tilt, the edges blur
with vibration

that rattles
the ocular nerve riding rough-shod
in the cranium

and shakes and carbonates
the cider barrel ribbed
under us

(for you've been feeding her apples)

as do blur the proprietary bounds
of here and there,
you and me

as there is heavy breathing,
yours or mine,
I cannot tell.

39

Times there is a getting on,
the leap of bass who from
the sea-grass of the basin
chase the sun's last flicker
and match its going down
with arc and tremulous splash.

Times there is a staying on
mossy softness to a trunk
or to the forest whole,
with rooting tentacles
clutched and mooring
in sweetness and in shadow.

Times there are for running hills
times for running still,
times for syrup to fill the cup
(full-bodied and with legging)
gives the horses juice they need
for gamboling and racing.

Times there is that slow greedy rock
leather saddles creaking,
horses on their low-gear way
down the valley edging.

Times there is a throwing over
would break most anyone's back.

Times, I know, if given the go,
we'd do it all again.

40

There are still points off radar
only blue horses can take you

out from the auks and cormorants
and all the deep water petrels

where you might probe for pearls
in the shells of seabeds

or catapult the firmament skeins,
cumulus or cirrostratus,

to marvel newborn jewels
bedecked in galactic cribs.

You might connect the dots
of archipelagoes

or rove with steenboks on the lam,
or swim with naiads

in the foaming brooks
that buck across the polished stones.

Airs above ground, or tangos high tide,
clip-clop on metamorphic rocks,

the blue horses tend from what is known
toward mystery

and pack us beyond what we've seen
and touched:

boxes of cattails and rose apples for lunch,
baked yellow pine cones picked young,

and koumiss
from the new dam.

41

Some days tend toward pilgrimage
you can't write home about,
mud fever and sweet itch,
the whole caravan lashed with doubt,
windgalls and fall sores, burden-packs, too,
pressing us low.

With every new plateau and berth,
hostile sands to counter,
gnarled carcasses, toothless skulls,
and buzzards dipping their beaks
in knowing motion.

Barren soil, cursed soil,
bitter *terra formidabala*
where we race an ever-lengthening course
a week or more outpaced,
with slippery troves and gleaming kernels
on slopes too steep to climb.

Nights, we find the safe houses
(reservations still honored)
vexed by the snarly-headed gorgon,
her camouflaged crates unhinged
and all the ubiquitous, coiled what-ifs
rattling in the corners.
On their agenda, our blood, my friend,

red cells in our marrow,
nothing less than iron-rich drops
to satisfy collateral.

Labyrinth of the loosening years
notched with fear and peril,
narrow the path, with no clear route,
no light nor even water,
for here, even horse-glow dims,
and knotted grows the thin rope
we thread to lead us through.

Woe to us, ill-fated pair,
when blue horses bear us
cobbled streets we dare not tread,
parade where slowly steps
a riderless horse
one eye back to all the years,
all the pleasure and the rubble,
the other tuned to what's ahead,
empty boots and puddled silence,
and barren stretches yet to cross, alone.

Would be one thing to gaze and go,
leaving behind the worst,
but the blue horses meander
and graze the sulking edges,
weave us through the hollow chambers
where brood the dolorous echoes.

In all, both crushing and salving hours,
let us keep saddle and ride.

42

Nights I know I've heard the horses
neighing at the bloody moon.
What solace for us is there then?

43

Comes comfort in the liniment
rubbed on and rubbing
wound-mending, ache-tending
simple comb and grooming
scent of eucalyptus blooming
slim cannons, knobby hocks
withers and quarters and loins,
shoulders and trembling flanks,
the blue glaze of all my pretty lot,
joint and ligament, tendon easing
sloughing off of a day's hard run
night and day and extra night,
quiet cosseting, pigeon-purring,
soothing of pain in clavicle and scapula,
humerus and all the residual sites
of ache crouching bone-deep.

Comes comfort in the muzzle
occasional but certain
cordate whorl of cowlick
edge of parted forelock
scrap of trust brought round at last,
forehead pressing sternum
a way you wouldn't expect
after all that cagey business
and muck. But here
there is nuzzle, here

the deep intake of breath,
here, the still taking
and just holding,
here, the keeping
secrets whispered
just a second,
then another,
in the lungs and near the heart.

Comes comfort in the heat,
the nighttime heat of horses,
and you.

Come, blue horses, all my pretty ones,
gather round and let me rub,
down and up, all the liniment in my cup.

Come, my rider, rounder of horses,
lie beside and let me rub
all the liniment from my cup.

44

Tonight, I sing of blue horses
and the periwinkle haze of a swollen moon
the hammering of hoof and surf and heart
mercurial dash across scalloped sands
and giving the reins.

I sing of blue horses to the hilt
in tides, eternal strokes from shore
slippery like so many flashing eels
moonlight glint on their haunches
bully current pushing against them
and all of us plowing through.

I sing of the short night and sleep not coming.
I sing of sleep not needing to come.

I sing of them striding flat out and back
stretching their formidable legs
planed out and planing still
cocksure in their soaring propulsion,
rocketbound.

I sing of slow mornings and blue horses
banded together, stamping, snorting,
shaking their heads, tossing off
pre-dawn jitters, hearts pulsing,
waiting the first slim fingers of sun.

Of the passage and heading out,
the jounce atop their brawny backs,
all of us fully fed
but you and I
and the blue horses
hungry to run.

I sing of blue coursers chomping the bit,
chewing up turf, gobbling
and swallowing the furlong,
scoffing the leaders, the bolt to finish ahead,
a neck, and a length of them.

I sing of long days off the circuit,
the maps uncharted, seams untapped,
and our small cavalcade
full of notion and intention.
I sing of vittles salted and smoked
and the rigging we do for the long haul.

I sing of missed meals
and meals not missed.
Of oasis and supplies.
Of bedding down
when the sun drops hard
and that lush range of forage
in dreamscape.

I sing of rest at valley's bottom
the sun now winking on wet hide

while we caress and murmur,
loosen the bridles, breastplates,
cruppers, caress the heads
and necks and shoulders,
offer barley and rye,
to these the bluest
apples of our eye.

I sing the desire
to never cease.

About the author:

A native of West Virginia, Lisa Graley is an assistant professor at The University of Louisiana at Lafayette where she teaches English and humanities. She has published in *Glimmer Train Stories*, *Water~Stone Review*, and *The McNeese Review*. The Louisiana Board of Regents awarded her an ATLAS (Awards to Louisiana Artists and Scholars) sabbatical in 2009-10 for her work in fiction..

More Poetry from Gival Press

12: Sonnets for the Zodiac by John Gosslee

Adama: Poème / Adama: Poem by Céline Zins with English translation by Peter Schulman

Bones Washed in Wine: Flint Shards from Sussex and Bliss by Jeff Mann

Box of Blue Horses by Lisa Graley

Camciones para una sola cuerda / Songs for a Single String by Jesús Gardea with English translation by Robert L. Giron

Dervish by Gerard Wozek

The Great Canopy by Paula Goldman

Grip by Yvette Neisser Moreno

Honey by Richard Carr

Let Orpheus Take Your Hand by George Klawitter

Metamorphosis of the Serpent God by Robert L. Giron

Museum of False Starts by Chip Livingston

On the Altar of Greece by Donna J. Gelagotis Lee

On the Tongue by Jeff Mann

The Nature Sonnets by Jill Williams

The Origin of the Milky Way by Barbara Louise Ungar

Poetic Voices Without Borders edited by Robert L. Giron

Poetic Voices Without Borders 2 edited by Robert L. Giron

Prosody in England and Elsewhere: A Comparative Approach by Leonardo Malcovati

Protection by Gregg Shapiro

Psaltery and Serpentines by Cecilia Martínez-Gil

Refugee by Vladimir Levchev

The Silent Art by Clifford Bernier

Songs for the Spirit by Robert L. Giron

Sweet to Burn by Beverly Burch

Tickets for a Closing Play by Janet I. Buck

Voyeur by Rich Murphy

Where a Poet Ought Not / Où c'qui faut pas by G. Tod Slone

For a complete list of Gival Press titles, visit: *www.givalpress.com*.

Books from Gival Press are available from Follett, major internet booksellers, your favorite bookstore, Internet, or directly from Gival Press at

Gival Press, LLC
PO Box 3812
Arlington, VA 22203
givalpress@yahoo.com
703.351.0079

www.ingramcontent.com/pod-product-compliance
Lightning Source LLC
Chambersburg PA
CBHW031202090426
42736CB00009B/758